KNOW JUSTICE
KNOW PEACE
WORKBOOK

UP Uriel Press
A DIVISION OF UMI

Scripture quotations are from the New King James Version Bible, English Standard Version Bible, The Message Version Bible, The Good News Translation Bible, and New International Version Bible.

Published in the United States by Uriel Press

P.O. Box 436987, Chicago, IL 60643

www.urielpress.com

ISBN: 979-8-9933670-1-9 (paperback)

Cover design by Laura Duffy

Printed in the United States of America

Contents

Getting Started

Welcome to the *Know Justice, Know Peace* Workbook experience. This workbook provides a biblical perspective on justice, rooted in God's character and His will for His people. Have you ever wondered why the justice journey and the important role of God's people in addressing injustice are seldom discussed in the church or bible colleges? Could it be that our land remains in need of healing because God's people shy away from seeking His face on this issue (2 Chronicles 7:14)? Are we capable of discerning between God's justice and our biases? Approaching justice from God's perspective allows us to face this issue without fear, inviting more power, love, and sound minds (2 Timothy 1:7). Expect healing and deliverance from misunderstanding what God's Word says about justice (Proverbs 4:7).

I am confident God is pleased with your decision to challenge yourself through individual study or enlighten others through small groups, congregational sermons, bible college curriculum, or online conversations. Expect to hear from God and receive revelation and insight!

The scriptures in this workbook are curated to invoke thoughtful reflections on justice, injustice, the heart of God, and our role as His people. Each chapter contains questions to promote self-reflection or healthy dialogue. Be prayerful about discerning between Biblical justice and human perspectives.

Here are tips for maximizing your experience:
If studying individually, work at your own pace but set a consistent schedule. Use the workbook as a daily devotion or a weekly chapter study. Write out your reflections and consider sharing insights on social media.

If facilitating a small group, work through the content prior to sessions and encourage each participant to have their own workbook. Establish an environment of respect and engagement. Allocate time for content discussion, activities, and prayer while fitting your needs.

Example session timeline (60 minutes):

- Open in prayer (5 min)
- Main leader recaps prior week, volunteers share insights (15 min)
- Main leader introduces chapter topic, shares stories, reviews scriptures (30 min)
- Table talk – small group discussion (25 min)
- Summary and insights from volunteers (10 min)
- Assign homework and close in prayer (5 min)

Note: For a 14-week study, alternate chapters between in-class and homework.

As Bible college curriculum, integrate workbook content into college coursework. Assign essays on chapter topics with personal reflections and practical applications.

As sermon content, adapt chapter topics for congregational sermons or a sermon series.

Whichever method you choose, trust that God has a life-changing revelation in store for you. Let your biblically-based justice journey begin!

Introduction

The tall, hulking black man stood curiously over the small robot, looking down as though mesmerized by the wheeled gadget. Drunk, he couldn't seem to figure it out or hear what "it" was saying to him. He had fallen asleep in someone's backyard before officers and a TV camera in a helicopter had located him. Awakened, he rolled onto his side revealing a pistol beneath him.

He pocketed the pistol during his robot encounter. He seemed to politely entertain the talk with the robot. He approached it, bending over to hear and speak. The drunken scene was far too funny just weeks after the killing of George Floyd in Minneapolis, but I could not contain my laughter. The conversation with the little robot finally led him to lay the gun down on the grass, make his way down the driveway, past a second robot, and compliantly into the arresting arms of law officers.

At least part of my glee, I'm sure, had to do with the favorable, less than brutal or deadly outcome of the encounter. Creative law enforcement had found a "dignified" way to encounter an American citizen!

The chant in every justice situation is "No justice -No Peace". we take it to a new level when we declare, "Know Justice-Know Peace". Enjoy leading and learning. Enjoy changing the world, one heart at a time.

CHAPTER 1

Know Justice, Know Peace

(Knowing the Word of God)

In recent years, discussions and debates about justice have been prevalent. The Church has both upheld and ignored justice at times. This reflection seeks to understand God's heart concerning justice

Does God care about Justice? (Yes or no) _____ If you answered "yes", why do you think God cares about justice?

_____

If you answered "no", why do you think God doesn't care about justice?

_____

Luke 11:42 ESV "But woe to you Pharisees! For you tithe mint and rue and every herb, and neglect justice and the love of God. These you ought to have done, without neglecting the others."

What do you think Jesus was saying in this verse?

_____

In what ways does the verse say that Christian's neglect justice?

_____

In what ways do Christian's neglect the "love of God"?

_____

CHAPTER 2

Know Justice, Know the Scriptures

In this passage of scripture, Jesus answers a question that has challenged religious leaders for thousands of years:

Matt. 22:35-40 NKJV And one of them, a lawyer, asked him a question to test him. **36** "Teacher, which is the great commandment in the Law?" **37** And he said to him, "You shall love the Lord your God with all your heart and with all your soul and with all your mind. **38** This is the great and first commandment. **39** And a second is like it: You shall love your neighbor as yourself. **40** On these two commandments depend on all the Law and the Prophets."

When the leader asked Jesus for "one" greatest commandment, why do you think Jesus gave him two commandments?

According to Jesus in Matthew 22:40, what is the significance of these two commandments in relation to all other commandments and teachings of the prophets?

Isaiah 61:8 ESV "For I the Lord love justice; I hate robbery and wrong; I will faithfully give them their recompense, and I will make an everlasting covenant with them."

What do you think God means when He says, "I, the Lord love justice "?

What does the Lord promise in terms of recompense for those wronged, according to Isaiah 61:8 ESV?

Luke 4:18-19 ESV "The Spirit of the Lord is upon me, because he has anointed me to proclaim good news to the poor. He has sent me to proclaim liberty to the captives and recovering of sight to the blind, to set at liberty those who are oppressed, to proclaim the year of the Lord's favor." The Lord Jesus made this bold proclamation when He introduced Himself in the synagogue as God's promised Christ. In this scripture which He read from a prophetic book written 700 years before His birth at Bethlehem, He outlines His earthly mission.

He listed four reasons for His coming, what are they?

_____

CHAPTER 3

Know Justice, Know Restoration

Isaiah 58:12 ESV And your ancient ruins shall be rebuilt, you shall raise up the foundations of many generations, you shall be called the repairer of the breach, the restorer of streets to dwell in.

Isaiah's prophetic ministry spanned the reigns of multiple Judean kings during the 8th century BCE. This was a tumultuous time, with the Assyrian Empire being the dominant force threatening the smaller nations, including the kingdoms of Israel and Judah. After rebuking the people for their insincere religious practices, God, through Isaiah, promises blessings for those who genuinely commit to righteousness and justice.

What might this passage be saying to you and to your generation?

What role does the verse describe in relation to "the foundations of many generations"?

What might the "breach" in "repairer of the breach" symbolize in a broader modern-day context?

What are the two titles given to the individual or group mentioned in the verse?

Isaiah 58:12 ESV is set against a backdrop of national spiritual decline, external religiosity without sincere commitment, and looming external threats. How does Isaiah 58:12 emphasize restoration and rebuilding in its message?

CHAPTER 4

Know Justice, Like Waters

(Knowing the heart of God)

Amo 5:10-13 NKJV They hate the one who rebukes in the gate, and they abhor the one who speaks uprightly. Amo 5:11 Therefore, because you tread down the poor and take grain taxes from him, though you have built houses of hewn stone, yet you shall not dwell in them; You have planted pleasant vineyards, But you shall not drink wine from them. Amo 5:12 For I Know your manifold transgressions and your mighty sins: Afflicting the just *and* taking bribes; Diverting the poor *from justice* at the gate. Amo 5:13 Therefore the prudent keep silent at that time, for it *is* an evil time.

In these verses Amos, demands justice in the affairs of men. The prophet condemns the men of Israel for the brutal treatment of the poor.

What is it they do to the poor?

———————————————

The word for "just" means law-abiding. What do they do to the "just"?

———————————————

Professor Paige H. Kelley wrote, "In ancient Israel, the courtroom was the open gate at the entrance to the walled city. There the elders of the city were seated as judges to rule on cases that were brought before them. (Amos 5:15; Ruth 4:1-12;) " Dr. Kelley wrote:

"In Amos' day, the trials were always rigged. The judges took bribes. The word used here for bribe is derived from a root meaning to cover. A bribe is covering money or hush money; the righteous, the innocent were never acquitted in these courts, but were afflicted, that is, treated as if they were guilty." "To turn aside the needy in the gate. "Simply means to deny them a fair trial. (In some cases, vigilantism, police, or otherwise). All the while God has been a silent witness to these transactions "for I Know your manifold transgressions, and your mighty sins…"[1]

Amo 5:24 But let justice run down like waters, And righteousness like a mighty stream.

Does this verse seem to teach that God wants justice to be permitted and plentiful?_____(Yes or No)

_____

Why do you think God wants justice to be plentiful?

_____

JUSTICE, LIKE WATERS

Chuck Swindoll has said," Support justice when you don't need it, and it will be there when you do."[2] Read the first 23 verses of Amos chapter 5.

How many times does Amos use the word justice?

_____

What does that seem to mean?

_____

How many times, in the 5th chapter, does Amos mention the poor?

_____

What might the poor have to do with justice?

_____

Is poverty usually a justice issue?

_____

What are some ways poverty could be a justice issue?

_____

Is it possible for religious people to get it wrong about God?

_____

How did God seem to feel about religion without justice?

_____

[1] denverjournal.denverseminary.edu and preachingsource.com
[2] azquotes.com and goodreads.com

Know Justice Know Peace Workbook

CHAPTER 5

Knowing The Human Heart

(The depth and heights of the heart of man)

Amy Vaughan was serving as an FBI intelligence analyst. She was nonetheless shocked when she discovered vulgar and hateful language from a man who passed as a regular citizen. Though she's white, the racist language was repulsive to her! Kristie Ronquille experienced the same phenomenon as a white woman attacked with the worst hateful, racist language. She, a respected member of the U.S. Coast Guard, had dated a black basketball player, and said of the same man, "He called me an n-word lover." Both surprised women testified at the trial of Travis McMichael, Gregory McMichael and William "Roddie" Bryan, in the brutal, sadistic, racist killing of black jogger Ahmaud Arberry. Both ladies were shocked by the racist language of the McMichaels and the hatred in their hearts. How can a heart hate so deeply? Whether in personal relationships or politics, how can people call wrong right and call right wrong? How can someone chase a stranger in the street and kill him. To quote Dr. Isaac Singleton, " the heart of the problem is the heart problem."

Jer 17:9 NKJV "The heart is deceitful above all things, and desperately wicked, Who can Know it?"

When you think of world history, what is the best thing you've heard/ seen of a human being doing?

_____

What is the worst thing you've ever heard of human beings doing?

_____

What do you think deceitful means?

_____

Is it possible for one to deceive oneself?

_____

Does this verse help your understanding of man's inhumanity to man?

_____

If it does, what does it tell you about injustice?

_____

THE HUMAN HEART

(The depth and heights of the heart of man cont.)

Isa 58:2 MSG They're busy, busy, busy at worship, and love studying all about me. To all appearances they're a nation of right-living people— law-abiding, God-honoring. They ask me, 'What's the right thing to do?' and love having me on their side.

Isa 58:3 MSG But they also complain, 'Why do we fast, and you don't look our way? Why do we humble ourselves and you don't even notice?' "Well, here's why: "The bottom line on your 'fast days' is profit. You drive your employees much too hard.

Isa 58:4 MSG You fast, but at the same time you bicker and fight. You fast, but you swing a mean fist. The kind of fasting you do won't get your prayers off the ground.

Isa 58:5 MSG Do you think this is the kind of fast day I'm after: a day to show off humility? To put on a pious long face and parade around solemnly in black. Do you call that fasting, a fast day that I, GOD, would like?

Isa 58:6 MSG «This is the kind of fast day I'm after: to break the chains of injustice, get rid of exploitation in the workplace, free the oppressed, cancel debts.

Isa 58:7 MSG What I'm interested in seeing you do is: sharing your food with the hungry, inviting the homeless poor into your homes, putting clothes on the shivering ill-clad, being available to your own families.

Isa 58:8 MSG Do this and the lights will turn on, and your lives will turn around at once. Your righteousness will pave your way. The GOD of glory will secure your passage.

Isa 58:9 MSG Then when you pray, GOD will answer. You'll call out for help, and I'll say, 'Here I am.' "If you get rid of unfair practices, quit blaming victims, quit gossiping about other people's sins,

Isa 58:10 MSG If you are generous with the hungry and start giving yourselves to the down-and-out, your lives will begin to glow in the darkness, your shadowed lives will be bathed in sunlight.

Is it possible for entire religious denominations (or even nations) to miss God altogether?

_____

What do these verses tell us about where or how Gods people went wrong?

_____

What did they seem to be doing right?

_____

Why did God reject their worship?

_____

CHAPTER 6

Knowing The Ways of the Unjust

Job 24:1 NKJV "Since times are not hidden from the Almighty, why do those who know Him see not His days?"

Job 24:2 NKJV "Some remove landmarks; They seize flocks violently and feed on them."

Job 24:3 NKJV "They drive away the donkey of the fatherless; They take the widow's ox as a pledge."

Job 24:4 NKJV "They push the needy off the road; All the poor of the land are forced to hide."

Psa 82:3 NKJV "Defend the poor and fatherless; Do justice to the afflicted and needy."

Mat 19:21 NKJV "Jesus said to him, "If you want to be perfect, go, sell what you have and give to the poor, and you will have treasure in heaven; and come, follow Me."

Jas 2:5 NKJV "Listen, my beloved brethren: Has God not chosen the poor of this world *to be* rich in faith and heirs of the kingdom which He promised to those who love Him?"

Jas 2:6 NKJV "But you have dishonored the poor man. Do not the rich oppress you and drag you into the courts?"

Do these passages seem to say that all poverty comes from laziness, or are there other forces that may cause poverty?

_____

What are some of the forces that may cause people to be poor?

_____

Name some ways we can do justice to the afflicted and needy. (Psalm 82:3)

_____

CHAPTER 7

Knowing God's Justice

How do these scriptures answer the following questions?

How does the concept of justice differ between the Old and New Testaments? (Exodus 21:23-25 vs Matthew 5:38-42)

What are some examples of God's justice and mercy in the Bible? (Genesis 18:16-33, Jonah 3-4, Romans 9:14-18)

How does the biblical idea of justice relate to the modern notions of human rights and social justice? (Micah 6:8, Isaiah 58:6-7, James 1:27)

How can Christian's practice justice in their personal and professional lives? (Colossians 3:23-25, Ephesians 4:28, Proverbs 31:8-9)

List four challenges and pitfalls of pursuing justice in a fallen world? (Ecclesiastes 4:1-3, Psalm 73, Habakkuk 1:2-4)

How does the gospel of Jesus Christ reveal God's justice and righteousness? (Romans 3:21-26, 2 Corinthians 5:21, Galatians 3:13-14)

How does the cross of Christ demonstrate both God's love and wrath? (John 3:16, Romans 5:8, Revelation 19:11-16)

How does the resurrection of Christ affirm God's justice and power over evil? (Acts 17:30-31, Romans 6:5-11, Revelation 20:11-15)

How does the Holy Spirit enable and empower Christians to live justly and righteously? (John 16:8-11, Galatians 5:16-26, Ephesians 5:8-10)

_____

_____

CHAPTER 8

Knowing How to Walk Your Justice

Review statements along with supporting paragraphs and scriptures. Ask God to apply important justice principles to areas of your life where you've experienced difficulties.

Biblical justice is based on God's eternal standard of goodness and rightness, rooted in Imago Dei (Gn 1:26). God is the only perfect, eternal, immovable standard for justice (Dt 32:4, Ps 9:1-2). All people are made in God's image, with dignity and immeasurable worth.

Human justice relies on the changing standards of morality and legality in human societies, influenced by culture, history, politics, and personal preferences. It often fails to recognize the inherent value and equality of all people, especially the marginalized and oppressed. **Isaiah**

5:20 (NIV): Woe to those who call evil good and good evil, who put darkness for light and light for darkness, who put bitter for sweet and sweet for bitter.

Biblical justice requires freedom, accountability, restoration, and transformation. It focuses not only on punishing wrongdoers but also on restoring victims and reconciling relationships. Aiming to bring God's shalom (peace) to the world, biblical justice is motivated by God's love and grace, empowering people to live according to His will and purpose. **Micah 6:8** (NIV): He has shown you, O mortal, what is good. And what does the Lord require of you? To act justly and to love mercy and to walk humbly with your God

Human justice demands compliance, retribution, compensation, and deterrence. It focuses on enforcing societal laws and rules, imposing penalties on lawbreakers, and restoring the status quo. Driven by human anger and fear, it often creates more resentment and violence. **Romans 13:1-4** (NIV): Let everyone be subject to the governing authorities, for there is no authority except that which God has established. The authorities that exist have been established by God. Consequently, whoever rebels against the authority is rebelling against what God has instituted, and those who do so will bring judgment on themselves. For rulers hold no terror for those who do right, but for those who do wrong. Do you want to be free from fear of the one in authority? Then do what is right and you will be commended. For the one in authority is God's servant for your good. But if you do wrong, be afraid, for rulers do not bear the sword for no reason. They are God's servants, agents of wrath to bring punishment on the wrongdoer

Biblical justice is revealed and fulfilled in Jesus Christ, the perfect embodiment of God's justice. He came to save the world from sin and death, demonstrating God's justice by healing the sick, feeding the hungry, forgiving sinners, and dying on the cross for our sake. Jesus invites us to follow Him and participate in His kingdom of justice and righteousness. **Colossians 1:15-20** (NIV): The Son is the image of the invisible God, the firstborn over all creation. For in him all things were created: things in heaven and on earth, visible and invisible, whether thrones or powers or rulers or authorities; all things have been created through him and for him. He is before all things, and in him all things hold together. And he is the head of the body, the church; he is the beginning and the firstborn from among the dead, so that in everything he might have the supremacy. For God was pleased to have all his fullness dwell in him, and through him to reconcile to himself all things, whether things on earth or things in heaven, by making peace through his blood, shed on the cross.

Human justice is challenged and transformed by Jesus Christ, the ultimate judge who will come again to judge the living and the dead. He exposed the hypocrisy and injustice of the religious and political authorities of his time, calling them to repent and believe. Jesus commands us to love God, love our neighbors as ourselves, and seek first His kingdom and justice. **Acts 17:30-31** (NIV): In the past God overlooked such ignorance, but now he commands all people everywhere to repent. For he has set a day when he will judge the world with justice by the man he has appointed. He has given proof of this to everyone by raising him from the dead.

Now that you have gained a better understanding of the differences between biblical justice and social justice; as well as how God reveals his character in justice and righteousness, read the scriptures below and answer the associated questions:

Read Isaiah 1:23; Amos 2:6,7; Micah 6:8 and Deuteronomy 14:28,29, and answer this question:

What are some examples of God's justice in action in the Old Testament?[3]

Read John 16:16-23; Matthew 16:21-23:24;1 John 3:8, and answer this question: How did Jesus demonstrate God's justice in his life, death, and resurrection?[4]

Read Micah 6:8; Isaiah 1:17; Galatians 5:22,23; John 16:13, and answer this question: How does the Holy Spirit empower us to pursue justice in our world today?[5]

Read Isaiah 1:17; Amos 5:24; Micah 6:8; Proverbs 31:8,9, and answer this question: What are some of the injustices that God cares about and wants us to address?[6]

---

[3] Grand Canyon University – Theology Thursday: Justice in the Old Testament
[4] Biblegateway.com
[5] Biblestudytools.com
[6] Lifehopeandtruth.com and biblestudytools.com

Read Romans 3:23; Proverbs 21:2; Proverbs 3:5,6; 1 Corinthians 2:14; James 1:5, and answer this question: How can we discern between God's justice and our own biases or preferences[7]?

_____

Read 1 Corinthians 2:14; James 1:5 answer this question: How can we balance justice and mercy in our relationships with others?[8]

_____

Read Psalm 122:6; Jeremiah 29:7; 1 Timothy 2:1,2; Isaiah 58:6; Micah 6:8 and answer this question: How can we pray for justice and peace in our communities and nations?[9]

_____

Read articles about Sojourners; Association for More Just Society; and World Vision, and answer this question: How can we partner with other Christians and organizations that are working for justice?

_____

Read scriptures Isaiah 59:14.15; Amos 5:12; Micah 7:2,3; Psalm 82:2,4; Proverbs 21:15 and answer this question: What are some of the challenges or obstacles that we may face when we seek justice[10]?

_____

Read scriptures Joshua 1:9; Psalm 27:1; Isaiah 41:10; 2Timothy 1:7; Philippians 4:13 and answer the following question: How can we overcome fear, apathy or discouragement in our pursuit of justice? [11]

_____

Read scriptures Colossians 3:12; Ephesians 4:32 Micah 6:8; Romans 12:15; Galatians 6:2; 1Peter 3:8, and answer the following question: How can we cultivate a heart of compassion and empathy for those who suffer injustice[12]?

_____

[7] Christianity.com
[8] Churchgists.com
[9] Praywithconfidence.com

Know Justice Know Peace Workbook

CHAPTER 9

Knowing True Worship

Who are these nameless ashen souls stacked like cordwood on the shelves of wooden Guineamen ships? Who were these bodies lifted from home, transported across mysterious seas, by people unknown, criminal oppressors by human standards, who demanded the captives learn quickly, a foreign language under threat of death? Who are these who soon realized the uncertainty of life and the future, for themselves or their kidnapped children? Would we forget their faces, would that we never saw. Would it not be more convenient to forget their anguished cry? In our collective consciousness, it hurts to think of it. Wouldn't it feel better to forget? To forget grief, which lasted so long? Most didn't die quickly; they were anguished, often confused, until death. For two hundred years, some 15-17 million people were uprooted from the freedoms of home. As many as 20% of them died en route to America. Many more were unlisted on ship manifests and records, in attempts to avoid governmental or financial inconvenience; therefore, their numbers were likely undercounted in historical reflections.

The whole world wrestles with the question. An entire culture and world are challenged to come to grips with this awful, uncomfortable, centuries-long event, too easy to track, too close to being a current event. It was indeed brutal.

Slavery ended 160 years ago.... didn't it? It was so sick that our national mentality begs to forget it, to forget them, to cyber past our wicked past. Couldn't they just remain nameless? Couldn't we just move on? There is no real value in discussing it, is there? Our children need not witness the sins of the nation's fathers, must they? The whole messy episode is forgettable, isn't it? The USA was a nation warned of its awful slaving and its greedy motives. no less a light than Charles Haddon Spurgeon, the most influential and powerful preacher of the 1800's, told of the sin of American slavery. He was rewarded with book burnings of his writings across the American south, and threats to his life. On February 17, 1860, citizens from Montgomery, Alabama, gathered in the jail yard to burn the "dangerous books" of Charles Haddon Spurgeon, the most popular Christian preacher in the Victorian world. A newspaper recorded the event:

"Last Saturday, we devoted to the flames a large number of copies of Spurgeon's Sermons…We trust that the works of the **greasy cockney vociferator** may receive the same treatment throughout the South. And if the Pharisaical author should ever show himself in these parts, we trust that a stout cord may speedily find its way around his eloquent throat."

A friend of Frederick Douglass, the London Pastor joined a growing chorus of abolitionists but found a deeply seated hatred, anger, and threats in America. Now, Spurgeon is widely quoted in American pulpits while Americans fight to forget the enslaved, he vouched for their freedom.[13] [14]

CHAPTER 10

Knowing The Way to Worship God

God is Spirit, and those who worship Him must worship in spirit and truth." John 4:24 (NKJV)

Read John 4:24. Is any kind of worship acceptable to God?

_____

What do you think Jesus meant when He gave the two ways that true worshippers would worship Him?

_____

Read Isaiah 58:2-6. Why do you think God cares about how we do justice "before" we worship Him?

_____

What might these words from Jesus have to do with it?

_____

Is it surprising to you that God cares so much about justice that He seems to interrupt their worship to demand it?

_____

Read verses 8-11 of this chapter, then list at least five things God promises to doers of justice.

{1}_____

{2}_____

{3}_____

{4}_____

{5}_____

Are there personal, spiritual benefits to doing justice?

_____

What are those benefits?

_____

In what ways might your life be better under those benefits?

_____

CHAPTER 11

Knowing How to Impress God

Matt 15:8 NKJV "These people draw near to me with their mouth, and honor me with their lips, but their heart is far from me.

Matt 15:9 NKJV And in vain they worship me, teaching as doctrines the commandments of men."

Jesus, here, is apparently not impressed even when one's words are right. He's not even satisfied when He's honored. Even worship can be "in vain".

What does Jesus seem to say is required to truly draw near Him?

_____

Pro 17:16 NKJV "Why *is there* in the hand of a fool the purchase price of wisdom, since *he has* no heart *for it?* "

What is the price of wisdom?

Psalms 12:2 NKJV "They speak idly everyone with his neighbor; *With* flattering lips *and* a double heart they speak. "

What do these verses have in common with Matt. 15:8,9 when describing the origin of sin?

_____

Matt 5:8 NKJV "Blessed *are* the pure in heart, for they shall see God. "

What is promised here, for the "pure in heart"?

_____

Rom 2:5 NKJV But in accordance with your hardness and your impenitent heart you are treasuring up for yourself wrath in the day of wrath and revelation of the righteous judgment of God, ...

What does this verse promise for the wicked hearted person?

_____

CHAPTER 12

Knowing The Price of Pride

"I never thought in my lifetime I would see Richmond and Charlottesville get rid of their statues. They're idols of white supremacy and symbols of racism and hate. And for me as a Christian, and many other faiths feel this way too, we can't have idols in our public square. That just doesn't square right with what we're trying to do as a community, as a state, a commonwealth or a nation."[15]

~ Robert W. Lee

Hos 13:6 NKJV "When they had pasture, they were filled; They were filled, and their heart was exalted; Therefore, they forgot Me."

Let us look at this verse from a more modern translation, then answer the question.

Here is the Good News translation: "Hos.13:6 But when you entered the good land, you became full and satisfied, and then you grew proud and forgot me."

What do you think caused them to forget God?

_____

How can one avoid the pride of heart that leads to separation from God?

_____

Read James 2:1-9 GNT

"**1** My friends, as believers in our Lord Jesus Christ, the Lord of glory, you must never treat people in different ways according to their outward appearance. **2** Suppose a rich man wearing gold ring and fine clothes comes to your meeting, and a poor man in ragged clothes also comes. **3** If you show more respect

[15] Robert W. Lee, descendant of Confederate General Robert E. Lee, author, "A Sin By Any Other Name." NPR Interview on April 2, 2019.

to the well-dressed man and say to him, "Have this best seat here," but say to the poor man, "Stand over there, or sit here on the floor by my feet," **4** then you are guilty of creating distinctions among yourselves and of making judgments based on evil motives.

5 Listen, my dear friends! God chose the poor people of this world to be rich in faith and to possess the kingdom which he promised to those who love him. **6** But you dishonor the poor! Who are the ones who oppress you and drag you before the judges? The rich! **7** They are the ones who speak evil of that good name which has been given to you.

8 You will be doing the right thing if you obey the law of the Kingdom, which is found in the scripture, "Love your neighbor as you love yourself." **9** But if you treat people according to their outward appearance, you are guilty of sin,

and the Law condemns you as a lawbreaker."

- Some were trained to dislike or treat people unfairly or discriminate?

- Some were trained to believe that "others" should be treated as less than oneself ?

- How can one change their heart if those they have loved and respected taught them differently from what God's Word teaches?

- What can one do if this is what they have learned?

_____

Mat 5:8 NKJV "Blessed *are* the pure in heart, for they shall see God." Can a rich or proud man be pure in heart?

_____

CHAPTER 13

Knowing My Pain

Rev.6:9 NKJV When He opened the fifth seal, I saw under the altar the souls of those who had been slain for the word of God and for the testimony which they held.

Rev 6:10 NKJV And they cried with a loud voice, saying, «How long, O Lord, holy and true, until You judge and avenge our blood on those who dwell on the earth?»

Rev 6:11 NKJV Then a white robe was given to each of them; and it was said to them that they should rest a little while longer, until both *the number of* their fellow servants and their brethren, who would be killed as they *were,* was completed.

- Wouldn't you think that when you finally get to Heaven that nothing else matters?
- Wouldn't it seem that once arriving at Gods throne, that you wouldn't care what others did to you on earth?
- Why would you think these believers were "crying "out to God to avenge their blood and take revenge on their murderers?
- _____

Which of these reasons would explain why God, in Heaven, said He would avenge them?

God is the God of Justice. _____ (Yes or No)

God wanted them to stop their protest.

_____

So, they could get out from under the throne?

_____

God has to balance the scales of Justice even in eternity

_____

CHAPTER 14

Knowing The Injustice of Man

"If you are neutral in situations of injustice, you have chosen the side of the oppressor."
– Desmond Tutu

Judges 6:3 NKJV So it was, whenever Israel had sown, Midianites would come up; also, Amalekites and the people of the East would come up against them.

Judges 6:4 NKJV Then they would encamp against them and destroy the produce of the earth as far as Gaza, and leave no sustenance for Israel, neither sheep nor ox nor donkey.

Judges 6:5 NKJV For they would come up with their livestock and their tents, coming in as numerous as locusts; both they and their camels were without number; and they would enter the land to destroy it.

Judges 6:6 NKJV So Israel was greatly impoverished because of the Midianites, and the children of Israel cried out to the LORD.

Judges 6:7 NKJV And it came to pass, when the children of Israel cried out to the LORD because of the Midianites,

Judges 6:8 NKJV that the LORD sent a prophet to the children of Israel, who said to them, "Thus says the LORD God of Israel: 'I brought you up from Egypt and brought you out of the house of bondage.

Was Gideon the Prophet in verse 8?

_____

If not, then who?

_____

Judges 6:9 NKJV and I delivered you out of the hand of the Egyptians and out of the hand of all who oppressed you, and drove them out before you and gave you, their land.

Was the poverty of Israel caused by their laziness?

_____

Why do you think these enemies would ruin the works of Gods people?

_____

Could such a thing happen Today?

_____

In what ways might that be happening in the 21st century?

_____

Jer 17:9 NKJV «The heart *is* deceitful above all *things,* and desperately wicked; Who can Know it? Does this verse help your understanding of man's inhumanity to man?

_____

If it does, what does it tell you about injustice?

_____

CHAPTER 15

Knowing Injustice

Injustice in the world refers to a lack of fairness, manifesting as social, economic, political, legal, and environmental injustices.

Is injustice in the world the same as injustice in the Bible?

___

Biblically, how do we NOT become practitioners of injustice?

___

Lev 19:15 NKJV ‹You shall do no injustice in judgment. You shall not be partial to the poor, nor honor the person of the mighty. In righteousness you shall judge your neighbor.

In making a judgment, to whom shall we give honor?

    a. A poor friend that we Know is an honorable person.

    b. A rich man who has offered me my perfect job..

    c. My brother just won the lottery.

    d. A homeless mother who needs to get off the streets.

    e. None of the above

Why might the verse specifically mention not being partial to the poor or deferring to the great?

___

What does the verse instruct about showing partiality in judgment?

___

Zep 3:5 ESV "The LORD within her is righteous; he does no injustice; every morning he shows forth his justice; each dawn he does not fail; but the unjust Knows no shame."

Who is "her" in Zep 3:5?

    a. God

    b. Jerusalem

    c. Judah

    d. Ninevah

Rom 9:14 ESV What shall we say then? Is there injustice on God›s part? By no means!

If we have undeniable evidence that God has injustice, how do we solve that problem?

_____

CHAPTER 16

Knowing What To Do

...Knowing the least of these...

Mat 25:35 NKJV for I was hungry, and you gave Me food; I was thirsty, and you gave Me drink; I was a stranger and you took Me in;

Mat 25:36 NKJV I *was* naked, and you clothed Me; I was sick, and you visited Me; I was in prison, and you came to Me.'

What do the classes of people listed by Jesus have in common?

_____

What are traditional ways which you may Know or have heard about to address each of these groups named?

_____

In Matthew 25:35, Jesus made the needy and poor Himself, in that verse. What does that say about God's heart for the destitute and abused?

_____

What would this verse seem to say is the best way to get to Jesus?

_____

"Justice will not be served until those who are unaffected are as outraged as those who are."
– Benjamin Franklin

"Ah! poor negro slave, every scar upon your back shall have a stripe of honor in heaven."
– Charles Haddon Spurgeon

CHAPTER 17

Knowing Outrage

Psalms 82:3 NKJV Defend the poor and fatherless; Do justice to the afflicted and needy.

In this verse the word ..."justice" is tsâdaq (tsaw dak). This word often means, "to make right". Sometimes it's translated, "to cleanse". When you think of the need for justice in your city or country, how does either meaning affect what you are seeing?

Do you believe you can commit your life to justice?

List at least three ways you can obey this verse.

Can we be outraged and still serve justice when injustice is being served and harbored by the people in power. Paul and Silas were arrested, dragged, tied up, stripped, beaten with rods, chained, feet put in stocks, and unfairly accused because of also being Jewish.

Can Paul and Silas be defended from this type of injustice?

What steps should someone who receives injustice like Paul and Silas take to be healed of this type of injustice?

CHAPTER 18

Knowing The Plan of God

Gal 2:7 MSG It was soon evident that God had entrusted me with the same message to the non-Jews as Peter had been preaching to the Jews.

Gal 2:9 MSG Recognizing that my calling had been given by God, James, Peter, and John—the pillars of the church—shook hands with me and Barnabas, assigning us to a ministry to the non-Jews, while they continued to be responsible for reaching out to the Jews.

Gal 2:10 MSG The only additional thing they asked was that we remember the poor, and I was already eager to do that.

Many translations refer to this message, entrusted by God to Paul, as "the gospel." Read these two passages, then name at least 4 (or 5) things that make the gospel actually "the gospel"?

(1 Cor. 15: 1-6: Gal. 4:1-6)

[1]_____

[2]_____

[3]_____

[4]_____

[5]_____

Why do you suppose God assigned Peter and Paul to reach out to two diverse kinds of people with the same message?

_____

Do you have an opinion about how this message may have been structured to reach "non-Jews"?

_____

Though the key leaders approved the message of Paul, what was the one thing they insisted must be included?

_____

Do you understand why such an ordinary thing as poverty would be so important to God?

_____

How should a church respond to poverty?

_____

How can an individual respond to or help the poor?

_____

CHAPTER 19

Knowing Biblical Justice in Society

Are our Christian standards the same as the world's? Can we be good citizens yet miss the mark with God? The Pharisees, religious leaders in the New Testament, were known for their strict observance of Jewish laws. Yet, Jesus criticized them for neglecting the more important aspects of the law: 'justice, mercy, and faithfulness' (Matthew 23:23, ESV). This suggests that even those who are externally righteous and perform good deeds can miss the heart of what God desires. While philanthropy and good deeds align with biblical principles, Christian teachings emphasize the importance of a personal relationship with God, repentance, and faith in Jesus Christ. Good works alone, without faith and a right heart towards God, might be seen as missing the mark in Christian theology.

How does the biblical instruction of "loving your neighbor" influence our society's understanding of justice? (Mark 12:31)

In what ways does today's justice system mirror the biblical principle of impartiality in judgment? (Leviticus 19:15)

How does the societal shift towards restorative justice align with the teachings of reconciliation in the Bible? (2 Corinthians 5:18-19)

How does our society protect the rights of the marginalized compared to biblical exhortations? (Psalm 82:3)

How do modern labor laws reflect the biblical teachings about fair wages? (James 5:4)

_____

In what ways does the Bible's emphasis on truth-seeking challenge our justice system? (Proverbs 12:17)

_____

CHAPTER 20

Knowing Biblical Justice and the Laws

The prophets, particularly in the Old Testament, frequently spoke against the rich oppressing the poor or denying them justice (e.g., Amos 5:11-12). Dishonesty using false measures, deceit in trade, or bribery is condemned (e.g., Deuteronomy 25:13-16). Showing favoritism or partiality, especially in judgment, is considered unjust (e.g., Leviticus 19:15). Taking advantage of the vulnerable or using exploitation: such as widows, orphans, and foreigners, is repeatedly condemned (e.g., Zechariah 7:10). Committing acts of violence such as rape, robbery, kidnapping, aggravated assault, battery, slavery or shedding innocent blood is seen as an abomination (e.g., Proverbs 6:16-19).

How does the biblical command to defend the rights of the poor and needy manifest in our society's welfare systems? (Proverbs 31:8-9)

How does our society's understanding of environmental justice mirror biblical stewardship of the earth? (Genesis 2:15)

Do modern concepts of community responsibility align with the biblical idea of bearing one another's burdens? (Galatians 6:2)

In what ways does our society's penal system reflect the biblical principle of "an eye for an eye"? (Exodus 21:24)

How do modern social movements advocating for the oppressed reflect biblical calls for justice?
(Isaiah 1:17)

_____

How do our societal views on debt relief relate to biblical practices like the Year of Jubilee?
(Leviticus 25:10)

_____

CHAPTER 21

Knowing God's Answer to Discrimination

Many religious individuals and groups recognize racial injustice as a violation of God's principle that all humans are created in His image and are of equal worth and dignity. To obey God's justice, they advocate for racial equality, participate in peaceful protests, and educate others about racial issues. Non-Government Organizations (NGOs) have created or collaborated with programs to support communities disproportionately affected by racial discrimination, providing educational resources, financial support, and safe spaces for dialogue. Consequently, many individuals examine their own biases, seek spiritual guidance to overcome them, and listen to those who have experienced racial discrimination, aiming to be allies and promote justice in their communities.

What does the Bible say about showing partiality based on wealth or social status? (James 2:1-4 (ESV)

What does the Old Testament teach about treating foreigners? (Leviticus 19:34 (ESV)

How does the Bible emphasize that all humans have equal value in the eyes of God? (Genesis 1:27 (ESV)

What does the New Testament teach about the unity of all believers, regardless of race or social status? (Galatians 3:28 (ESV)

How did Jesus challenge societal discrimination during His ministry? (John 4:9 (ESV)

How does the Bible address discrimination within the church community? (1 Corinthians 12:12-13 (ESV)

_____

_____

What does the Bible say about justice and defending the rights of the marginalized?
(Proverbs 31:8-9 (ESV

_____

CHAPTER 22

Know How to Love Mercy

In the Bible, equity means treating individuals fairly, considering their unique circumstances. Righteousness involves living according to God's laws and is intrinsic to God's nature. Justice emphasizes fair judgment and protecting the vulnerable. While the Bible doesn't use the term 'crisis response,' leaders and prophets often acted in the face of challenges, like Joseph during the famine in Egypt (Genesis 41). Although equity, righteousness, justice, and crisis response can intersect, especially in ethics and morality, they are distinct concepts with unique implication.

How does God respond to the prayers of the righteous during crises? (Proverbs 15:29 (ESV)

_____

How are righteousness and equity related in Proverbs? (Proverbs 21:5 (ESV)

_____

What are the implications of injustice on a society? (Proverbs 21:15 (ESV)

_____

What does the Bible say about equal treatment in the community? (Leviticus 24:22 (ESV)

_____

How should we respond when we see someone in crisis? (Galatians 6:2 (ESV)

_____

How are we to act justly and love mercy? (Micah 6:8 (ESV)

_____

CHAPTER 23

Knowing Justice in Society

Social Injustice: This relates to discrimination or prejudice based on race, gender, age, economic status, religion, nationality, or other societal constructs. It results in certain groups being marginalized, oppressed, or denied basic rights and opportunities.

Economic Injustice: This form of injustice is seen when resources and wealth are unevenly distributed, often due to systems that favor a particular class or group at the expense of others.

Political Injustice: When those in power use their position to benefit themselves or a particular group disproportionately, often suppressing opposition or the rights of minorities.

Legal Injustice: This occurs when laws are applied unevenly or are biased against certain groups, or when the judicial system fails to uphold the rights of individuals.

Environmental Injustice: This can be observed when certain communities face disproportionate exposure to pollutants or environmental hazards, often because they lack the economic or political power to advocate for themselves.

How does societal justice differ from biblical justice? (Micah 6:8)

_____

What role does mercy play in biblical justice compared to societal justice? (Matthew 5:7)

_____

In what ways does society reward or punish just behavior? How does the Bible view rewards for justice? (Matthew 25:34-40)

_____

How does the Bible define justice for the marginalized? How does society approach it? (Psalm 82:3)

_____

How do societal laws on retribution compare with the "eye for an eye" principle in the Old Testament? (Leviticus 24:20)

_____

How does society view forgiveness in justice systems versus biblical teachings on forgiveness? (Matthew 18:21-22)

_____

CHAPTER 24

Knowing Justice and the Church

How is equity related to righteousness in Proverbs?
(Proverbs 16:11 ESV)

What does the Bible say about
showing partiality in judgment?
(Deuteronomy 1:17 ESV)

What does the Bible say about
equity in recompense?
(Romans 12:20 ESV)

How does the Bible advise dealing
with debt and the poor?
(Leviticus 25:35 ESV)

What does the Old Testament law
say about equal punishment?
(Exodus 21:24-25 ESV)

How are the Israelites instructed to
treat foreigners?
(Leviticus 19:34 ESV)

What does the New Testament say
about equal punishment?
(Matthew 5:38-40 ESV)

CHAPTER 25

Knowing Equity

What does the Bible say about partiality in court?
(Deuteronomy 16:19 ESV)

What does Proverbs say about favoring the rich?
(Proverbs 22:16 ESV)

How does God view diverse weights and measures?
(Proverbs 20:10 ESV)

What does the Bible say about justice? (Isaiah 1:17 ESV)

How are believers instructed to regard others?
(Philippians 2:3 ESV)

What does the Bible say about treating others as we'd like to be treated? (Matthew 7:12 ESV)

CHAPTER 26

Knowing How to Be Like God

What does the Bible say about
responding to the needs of the poor
in times of crisis?
(Leviticus 25:35 (ESV)

How does the Bible depict justice
and righteousness in society?
(Psalm 89:14 (ESV)

How does the Lord view unjust
scales or measures?
(Proverbs 11:1 (ESV)

How should we respond when we
see injustice?
(Isaiah 1:17 (ESV)

What does the Bible say about partiality in judgment? (Leviticus 19:15
(ESV)

In times of crisis, what attitude
should we have towards our
resources? (Matthew 5:42 (ESV)

CHAPTER 27

Knowing Justice in the Power of the Cross

How does the cross of Christ demonstrate both God's love and wrath? (John 3:16, Romans 5:8, Revelation 19:11-16)

How does the resurrection of Christ affirm God's justice and power over evil? (Acts 17:30-31, Romans 6:5-11, Revelation 20:11-15)

How does the Holy Spirit enable and empower Christians to live justly and righteously? (John 16:8-11, Galatians 5:16-26, Ephesians 5:8-10)

How does the church as the body of Christ reflect God's justice and grace to the world? (Matthew 5:13-16, Ephesians 2:11-22, 1 Peter 2:9-12)

How does the church as the bride of Christ anticipate God's final judgment and restoration? (Matthew 25:31-46, Revelation 21:1-8, Revelation 22:12-17)

How should Christians respond to injustice and oppression in their own contexts and cultures? (Luke 10:25-37, Romans 12:9-21, Philippians 2:1-11)

CHAPTER 28

Knowing Crisis Response

When Jonah was in the belly of the fish, what was his response? (Jonah 2:1-9 ESV)

_____

How did Job respond to the devastating news of losing his family and property? (Job 1:20-21 ESV)

_____

What did the Lord instruct the Israelites to do when faced with the crisis of the advancing Egyptian army at the Red Sea? (Exodus 14:16 ESV)

_____

How did David react when he heard of Saul's death? (2 Samuel 1:11-12 ESV)

_____

When King Hezekiah was told he would die from his illness, how did he respond? (2 Kings 20:2-3 ESV)

_____

How did Mordecai and the Jews in Susa react to King Ahasuerus's decree to destroy the Jews? (Esther 4:1-3 ESV)

_____

When Peter saw Jesus walking on the water, he began to sink, what did he do? (Matthew 14:30 ESV)

_____

NKJV "And in vain they worship me, teaching as doctrines the commandments of men."

Jesus, here, is apparently not impressed even when one's words are right. He's not even satisfied when He's honored. Even worship can be "in vain".

What does Jesus seem to say is required to truly draw near Him?

_____

Pro 17:16 NKJV "Why *is there* in the hand of a fool the purchase price of wisdom, since *he has* no heart *for it?* "

What is the price of wisdom?

_____

Psalms 12:2 NKJV "They speak idly everyone with his neighbor; *With* flattering lips *and* a double heart they speak. "

What do these verses have in common with Matt. 15:8,9 when describing the origin of sin?

_____

Matt 5:8 NKJV "Blessed *are* the pure in heart, for they shall see God. "

What is promised here, for the "pure in heart"?

_____

Rom 2:5 NKJV But in accordance with your hardness and your impenitent heart you are treasuring up for yourself wrath in the day of wrath and revelation of the righteous judgment of God, ...

What does this verse promise for the wicked-hearted person?

_____

Bibliography

[1] denverjournal.denverseminary.edu and preachingsource.com

[2] azquotes.com and goodreads.com

[3] Robert W. Lee, descendant of Confederate General Robert E. Lee, author, "A Sin By Any Other Name." NPR Interview on April 2, 2019.

[4] The Christian Watchman & Reflector 19th Century Boston Baptist Newspaper: Article by Rev. C.H. Spurgeon, September 27, 1860. Article by Rev. C.H. Spurgeon, August 23, 1860.

[5] https://www.spurgeon.org/resource-library/blog-entries/the-reason-why-america-burned-spurgeons-sermons-and-sought-to-kill-him/

[6] Why Social Justice is not Biblical Justice by Scott David Allen

[7] God's Justice vs. Human Justice by Morgan Guyton

[8] thewitness.org

[9] Grand Canyon University – Theology Thursday: Justice in the Old Testament

[10] Biblegateway.com

[11] Biblestudytools.com

[12] Lifehopeandtruth.com and biblestudytools.com

[13] Christianity.com

[14] Churchgists.com

[15] Praywithconfidence.com

[16] gsdrc.org and universalhumanrightsindex.org

[17] Bible.knowing-jesus.com and biblestudytools.com

[18] Bible.knowing-Jesus.com and bing.com

Disclaimer

This document is intended to provide a biblical perspective on justice, which is rooted in God's character and His will for His people. It does not address specific legal issues or cases, nor does it advocate for any form of retribution or violence against those who commit injustice. The reader is advised to consult other sources for such matters and to exercise discernment and wisdom in applying the principles of biblical justice to their own context.

www.ingramcontent.com/pod-product-compliance
Lightning Source LLC
Chambersburg PA
CBHW070651130626
46555CB00006B/2811